Recapitalization of Banks in Transition Economies:

Poland and Hungary in the New Market Economy

By

James C. Mitchell, Jr.

ISBN: 1-4107-4969-X (e-book)
ISBN: 1-4107-4968-1 (Paperback)

Library of Congress Control Number: 2003093586

This book is printed on acid free paper.

Printed in the United States of America
Bloomington, IN

1stBooks - rev. 07/05/03

AD MAJOREM DEI GLORIAM

TO MY PARENTS

Introduction

'Probably in no other domain are the organizing principles of the Soviet-style central planning and of the capitalist market economy so radically opposed as in matters of finance.'[1]

'Across the great landmass from Brandenburg to the Bering Straits the business of banking is reviving, as market economies are established. A process that took hundreds of years in Western Europe and decades in Japan is being telescoped into a few years in Central and Eastern Europe and the Former Soviet Union.'[2]

These two observations underscore the significant magnitude and crushing time constraints of transition banking in Central and Eastern Europe (CEE). In the decade following the collapse of communism, Poland and Hungary emerged as two of the region's economic leaders. Both countries are consequently poised as early candidates to join the European Union. Although not finalized, the road to accession-readiness was paved through the bitter economic and political landscape of the 1990s. The decade was ushered in by the requirements of economic reform on an unprecedented level. Starting virtually from scratch, the development of a financial structure was needed to underpin the economy. While a banking system existed under communism, it bore no resemblance to the type of institution required for a market economy.

Under the right conditions, financial markets and institutions allocate resources, 'intermediating between savers who seek safe and remunerative repositories for their funds and entrepreneurs seeking external finance for investment projects.'[3] They also support hard budget constraints by assessing projects on a risk and return basis, monitoring funds and holding corporate governance accountable. Transaction costs may be reduced because banks efficaciously manage monetary transfers and payments. According to the European Bank for Reconstruction and Development (EBRD), economic performance is determined by the efficiency of the financial institutions and markets.[4] Yet early in the transition, most governments primarily focused their attention on macroeconomic stabilization and price liberalization. It did not take long, however, before a crisis erupted in the banking system that threatened to undermine the entire economy.

The root of the crisis centered on the fledgling economies' banks holding both poor and non-performing loans. The governments of

Poland and Hungary responded with a series of measures in the early and mid 1990s that included the targeting of bad loans and recapitalization of banks. Their policy approaches, however, took divergent paths. Poland implemented decentralized loan recovery with hard budget constraints. Hungary pursued partially centralized loan recovery and practiced soft budget constraints. This paper analyzes the strengths and weaknesses of the two policies, while striving to discern an optimal recapitalization strategy.

Chapter 1 presents a brief overview of banking in transition countries. Common problems and unique challenges are highlighted, as well as the development of the two-tiered system and the vital linkages between the micro and macro economy. Chapter 2 delineates the key interdependent success factors of bank recapitalization. In addition to outlining the nature of the problem, this chapter establishes a theoretical and systematic framework for analyzing government policies. It affirms that a comprehensive approach to recapitalization is integrally related to success. The injection of capital into a banking system without carefully examining policy issues such as conditionality, regulation and supervision, enterprise restructuring, bankruptcy and privatization is a recipe for disaster. Chapters 3 and 4 analyze the approaches to bank recapitalization that were taken by Poland and Hungary, respectively. Direct and indirect costs and benefits are measured against the objectives established in the second chapter. The Conclusion underscores government's best (and worst) practices and policy optimization.

Notes

1 Ronald W. Anderson and Chantal Kegels: *Transition Banking, Financial Development of Central and Eastern Europe.* United States: Oxford University Press Inc., 1998, p.vii.
2 Jacek Rostowski: *Banking Reform in Central and Eastern Europe and the Former Soviet Union.* Budapest: Central European University Press, 1995, p.1.
3 European Bank for Reconstruction and Development: *Transition report 1998—Financial sector in transition.* United Kingdom: EBRD Publications, 1998, p.92.
4 IBID.

Acknowledgements

Pursuing an advanced degree at the London School of Economics allows one to interact with international scholars and world leaders on global issues. I am grateful to many people for giving me this rare and unique opportunity. The years of preparation and encouragement are almost solely the result of my parents' (Jim and Paula Mitchell) financial sacrifice and dedication to academic excellence. My sister and brother-in-law, Theresa and Dr. George Zainea, also provided support and financial resources. Aden Adams, Tom Schoenleben, Ray Sharp, Dan Green and other senior managers at CSX championed my corporate leave-of-absence and arranged the corporate financial package. They understood that 'people make the difference' are more than words on a value statement.

Family and friends provided support to make the one-year commute between the United States and the United Kingdom possible. Lori, James and Lauren managed to keep the household running smoothly in Florida despite hurricane threats and visits from the local wildlife. The continuous care-packages, calls and letters from mom, dad, Sharon, Tom, Theresa, Sarah, Tamara, the kids, et al., brightened up many overcast days in London. Jay Adams, Richard Burge and Ernie Thrasher kept me on the civilized side of London society. The Carlton Club, Fly Fishers' Club, Wilton's, London Symphony Orchestra, Middle Eastern cuisine and Cuban cigars really took the edge off of countless hours in the library.

The professors and international students at the LSE are world class. Nick Barr, a leading World Bank economist, said in an introductory lecture that the education one received at the pub would equal what was learned in the classroom. The George IV Club proved that he was correct; sometimes complex international problems are best analyzed over ale. Professors Barr, Innes, Wunner, Soskice, et al. and the students at the LSE European Institute made the year both challenging and enlightening.

This work could not have been accomplished without the guidance and direction of my tutor at the LSE, Norbert Wunner, and Jan Bielecki, the former Prime Minister of Poland. A gifted German economist, Dr. Wunner would accept nothing less than academic distinction. The candor and unparalleled insight of Prime Minister

Bielecki allowed me to transcend economic theory and truly comprehend the dynamics of decision-making in a financial crisis. I am also grateful to Dr. Martin Raiser and Libor Krkoska, economists at the European Bank for Reconstruction and Development.

To those that encouraged me to publish this book and to Becky Harling Price and Lev Slavin for editing it—thank you.

Shukran ABA

Contents

Introduction.. v

    Notes viii

Acknowledgements ix

Chapter 1. Transition Banking....................................... 1

    1.1 Common crises 1

    1.2 Evolution: from plan to market 2

    1.3 Measuring the problem.. 4

    1.4 Ripples in the system... 5

    Notes 6

Chapter 2. Interdependent Success Factors..................... 8

    2.1 Bad loans: stock and flow issues 8

    2.2 Conditional recapitalization 10

        2.2.1 The role of government............................. 10

        2.2.2 Conditionality... 14

    2.3 Regulation, supervision and enforcement 17

    2.4 Enterprise restructuring and bankruptcy 19

        2.4.1 Enterprise restructuring: banks' interests............... 19

        2.4.2 Bankruptcy policies................................... 21

    2.5 Privatization... 22

    Notes 24

Chapter 3. Poland **26**

   3.1   Organization and approach 26

   3.2   1993 law on financial restructuring 32

   3.3   Results 34

   Notes 37

Chapter 4. Hungary **38**

   4.1   Antecedents and developments 38

       4.1.1   Legacy 38

       4.1.2   Evolution and structure 39

       4.1.3   Laws, institutions and bankruptcy 42

   4.2   The loan consolidation schemes 44

   Notes 50

Conclusion **53**

   Notes 57

Bibliography **59**

Chapter 1

Transition Banking

1.1   Common crises

Financial crisis in the banking sector is by no means a unique
feature of transition economies.   International experience indicates
that incentive-based issues, such as regulatory forbearance, political
intervention to avoid collapses, unconditional bailouts, risky
investments, under-reporting of non-performing assets and extended
deposit insurance cause serious damage to financial discipline in
developed market economies.[1]   A recent article on U.S. banking in
The Economist warned '…lending standards are still loose, and it is
the loans that they made earlier that are likely to return to haunt
them.'[2]   This caveat comes on the heels of the 1980s U.S. Savings &
Loan scandal that cost American taxpayers hundreds of billions of
dollars: prompting Stiglitz's observation that, 'mistakes of this
magnitude are hard to fathom.'[3]   While banking crises are common to
both financially developed and developing countries, transition

economies have extra problematic dimensions. One source of the crisis originates from the past decisions of the state, leaving many of the current actors to shirk accountability.[4] Another issue concerns the distinction between risk and uncertainty. In the case of risk, the possible collections of outcomes and their probabilities are known; with uncertainty, outcomes and probabilities are mostly unknown.[5] Developed market economies exhibit more instances of the former, while unstable transition economies are much more prone to the latter.

1.2   Evolution: from plan to market

The early evolution of the banking system in transition economies took similar trajectories in most CEE countries. It involved splitting the old monobank into a two-tiered structure. Poland and Hungary were actually ahead of most countries in this regard, as the separation occurred prior to the transition. Under socialism, the monobank provided credit to enterprises as a function of the central plan. It essentially performed an accounting function. Commercial banking was nonexistent. Under the new reforms, the two-tiered structure created a Central Bank, which was primarily macroeconomic in nature, and separate commercial banks, which directly financed the economy.[6] This system, however, was still dominated by state ownership. A new, three-tiered structure, whereby co-operatives or joint stock companies were created, was intended to facilitate greater private ownership. In practice, most joint stock companies were owned by other banks and enterprises, which were also state-owned.[7] This early, incestuous pattern of state ownership provided a fertile environment for the mismanagement of problematic loans. Chapter 2 focuses on this issue in greater detail and outlines how properly structured recapitalization policies can influence behavioral change.

While the fledgling banking system looked structurally workable, buried in the bank's ledgers were ticking time bombs. The commercial banks that were hived off from the old monobank inherited a plethora of risky loans. It is important to remember that the monobank was a fountain of soft credit for enterprises under the old system. Transition brought price liberalization and economic reforms, as well as a reduction in overt government subsidies. This put great stress on the profitability (and liquidity) of many enterprises and fueled the bad loan dilemma.

1.3   Measuring the problem

'The balance sheets of commercial banks are virtually a mirror of the economic and commercial life of a country...poorly performing economies mean poorly performing loans.'[8] Early in the transition, banks were caught in a vicious cycle. They reacted to an unstable business environment and, at the same time, caused some of the instability. The key question is how to properly scope the magnitude of the interrelated macroeconomic situation and the debt issue. A good measurement tool is the (non-government) Credit/GDP ratio. 'Countries where credit, because of previous bad policies, is a relatively small portion of GDP...have less trouble than countries with larger credit/GDP ratios, [both of] which have to bail out their banks.'[9]   Using this evaluative criterion, there is a significant difference between Poland and Hungary: the former started with an approximate 20% credit/GDP ratio, while the latter topped-out at about 45%.[10] In sum, Hungary's reliance on credit was initially more than twice as large as the situation faced by Poland.

1.4   Ripples in the system

Bad loans are like cancer cells: if they are not stopped, the whole banking system may become infected.   Banks, enterprises and ultimately the economy become destabilized. Systemic bank failure 'can bring a drastic reduction in the banking system's ability to finance investment and consumer-durable expenditure, thus reducing aggregate demand and throwing the economy into a slump.'[11] While the impact of the interaction between the banking system and the macro economy is beyond the scope of this paper, a critical aspect of the bad loan problem and its relation to the economy is worth noting here. A standard indicator of pricing behavior and competitiveness is the interest rate spread,[12] the difference between a bank's lending rates and the cost of borrowing from the Central Bank. Banks had to increase their spreads to cover the non-performing loans (see end note #12 for the caveat). From the first quarter of 1992 to the fourth quarter of 1993 interest rate spreads jumped approximately 67% in

Poland and 80% in Hungary, reaching levels of 20% and 9%, respectively.[13] This created an adverse selection problem, as well-performing companies were forced to bear the higher cost of finance. Faced with a lack of alternative sources of credit, such as a developed equities market, some firms turned to foreign institutions rather than use domestic banks.[14] The bad loan problem clearly had to be addressed at the source rather than attempting to 'cope' with the problem afterwards.

Notes

1 European Bank for Reconstruction and Development: *Transition report—Financial sector in transition.* United Kingdom: EBRD Publications, 1998, p.133.
2 *The Economist,* 29 July 2000, p.83.
3 Joseph Stiglitz: *Whither Socialism?* Cambridge, Massachusetts: MIT Press, 1994, p.208.
4 John P. Bonin and Istvan P. Szekely: *The Development and Reform of Financial Systems in Central and Eastern Europe.* England: Edward Elgar Publishing Limited, 1994, p.2.
5 Willem H. Buiter, Ricardo Lago and Helen Rey: Financing transition: investing in enterprises during macroeconomic transition. EBRD Working Paper No. 35, December 1998, p.19.
6 www.nbp.pl/en/onbp/historia.html
7 Jenny Corbett and Colin Mayer: Financial Reform in Eastern Europe: Progress with the Wrong Model. *Oxford Review of Economic Policy,* Vol. 7, No. 4, ~1991, p.57.

8 Brian Quinn: Banking Supervision in the Transition Economy. In Steven Fries: Building sound banking in transition economies. EBRD Working Paper No. 17, April 1996, pp.22-23.

9 Kalman Mizsei: Lessons from Bad Loan Management in the East Central European Economic Transition for the Second Wave of Reform Countries. In Jacek Rostowski: *Banking Reform in Central and Eastern Europe and the Former Soviet Union.* Budapest: Central European University Press, 1995, p.59.

10 Libor Krkoska, Economist—EBRD, private interview on 28 July 2000 in London, England.

11 Paul Krugman and Maurice Obstfelt: *International Economics Theory and Policy.* Reading, Massachusetts: Addison-Wesley, 1997, p.667.

12 Istvan Abel and Istvan Szekely: Market Structures and Competition in the Hungarian Banking System. In Bonin & Szekely, 1994, p.278. Note: Interpreting interest rate spreads can be controversial in transition economies.

13 Peter Dittus (1994): Bank reform and behavior in Central Europe. *Journal of Comparative economics* 19: p.349.

14 Marie Lavigne: *The Economics of Transition—From Socialist Economy to Market Economy.* London: Macmillan Press Ltd., 1999, p.187.

Chapter 2

Interdependent Success Factors

2.1   Bad loans: stock and flow issues

Bad loans may be divided into stock and flow problems. The formers are non-performing assets carried over by state-owned enterprises under central planning. As outlined in Chapter 1, the radical impact of transition severely weakened the ability of many companies to service their debts. Inflation tends to mask these debts until stabilization takes hold. Then positive real interest rates exacerbate the loan problem.[1] The flow issue arises from the bank's later issuance of credit. 'Newly established banks were not prudent or experienced enough not to lend to non-viable firms while the lack of reforms in the old banks allowed them to continue their old habits.'[2] The key to successful bank recapitalization is to attack both the stock and flow problems on a once-off basis.

Identifying and isolating the stock of bad loans is essential. As long as bad debts remain on banks' books there is a continued likelihood for indirect government subsidies and credit pressure from weakened state-owned enterprises (SOEs), driving a capital crunch to the banks' bottom line. For example, laws may prohibit the overt subsidization of industries. Rolling over loans and capitalizing the interest, however, is an opaque way of keeping dinosaurs alive. If inherently troubled enterprises require government assistance (e.g., national interest, economic importance, 'too big to fail', etc.), it should come in the form of a transparent policy.[3] Early in the transition, banks' most important assets were the credits granted to state institutions. Banks are thus in a precarious position on calling loans or simply canceling debt since it would render them insolvent. In other words, the problem was just too big. Dittus estimated that by 1992/1993 overall bad loans had ballooned to 30% of banks' portfolios.[4] With bad loans threatening the capital base, banks' lending decisions became distorted. There was a strong incentive to finance high-risk deals, providing higher returns, to compensate for the at-risk capital. In sum, fundamental disequilibrium arose when incumbent SOEs dominated bank credit. Both the quantity and quality of lending was affected, leading to economic and financial harms, such as expensive credit, crowding out and deadweight losses.[5]

2.2   Conditional recapitalization

2.2.1   The role of government

The market forces causing the upheaval in transition economies are themselves unable to resolve the SOE and bad loan problems. Hamstrung by the old system's legacy, with weak legal and institutional frameworks, Adam Smith's invisible hand is tied. 'That is, a market solution, one that does not entail any intervention by the state, would result in the collapse of the payment and financial intermediation system.'[6]   The state must clearly intervene in the banking system.   Government policy interventions can take place either on the assets or liabilities side of a bank's ledger.   To improve the quality of assets, government securities may be swapped for the bad loans.   An important issue here is who ends up holding the debt (refer to the section on enterprise restructuring).   'Alternately, the state could intervene in order to assure the performance of the existing loan portfolio.   The second class of measure would work on the liability side of the ledger.'[7] Under the liability scenario, banks may receive capital infusions or access to low-cost funding (e.g., from the Central Bank).[8]

Government intervention in the economy; have we come full circle? Only if one considers the U.S. government's role in the Savings & Loan crisis as socialist. In transition economies the state plays a key role in introducing and strengthening prudential regulation and supervision, as well as the recapitalization and privatization of state banks. This does not mean that openness, prudence and arm-length relationships between politics and the financial and corporate sectors are necessarily compromised.[9]

In addition to struggling with the legacies of the past, governments face another formidable problem in resolving the banking crisis: namely money. State budgets are under tremendous strain during the transition. Government measures must therefore be extremely well calculated. Two objectives of recapitalization are boosting a bank's risk-weighted capital adequacy ratio (CAR) [10] and, very importantly, effectively managing the non-performing loans. Without fundamentally restructuring the loans, gains from a capital injection will be quickly eroded. This issue is addressed in the following section on conditionality.

The state is faced with a triage situation in determining eligibility for scarce recapitalization resources. Economic theory is relatively clear: 'the decision should be based primarily, but not solely, on the basis of financial and operational criteria that indicate potential viability.'[11] But in transition economies this criterion is not always workable or clear. Some banks may be weak but play a critical role in the economy, particularly a large bank, 'or one that dominates a region of the country, underpins the payment system, or has a special niche in the credit market.'[12] Chapter 3 provides a good example of Poland excluding specialized banks from the 'decentralized hard' approach. To increase the capital position of banks, the International Monetary Fund's (IMF) parameters on recapitalization targets are instructive. Banks are essentially classified into four categories [fig. 2.1]: (A)—capable of surviving without public money, (B) and (C)— recovery with government assistance, and (D)—unlikely to recover.[13] The objective is to strategically strengthen and maintain the CAR by the recovery phase. In transition economies, however, many banks

Fig. 2.1

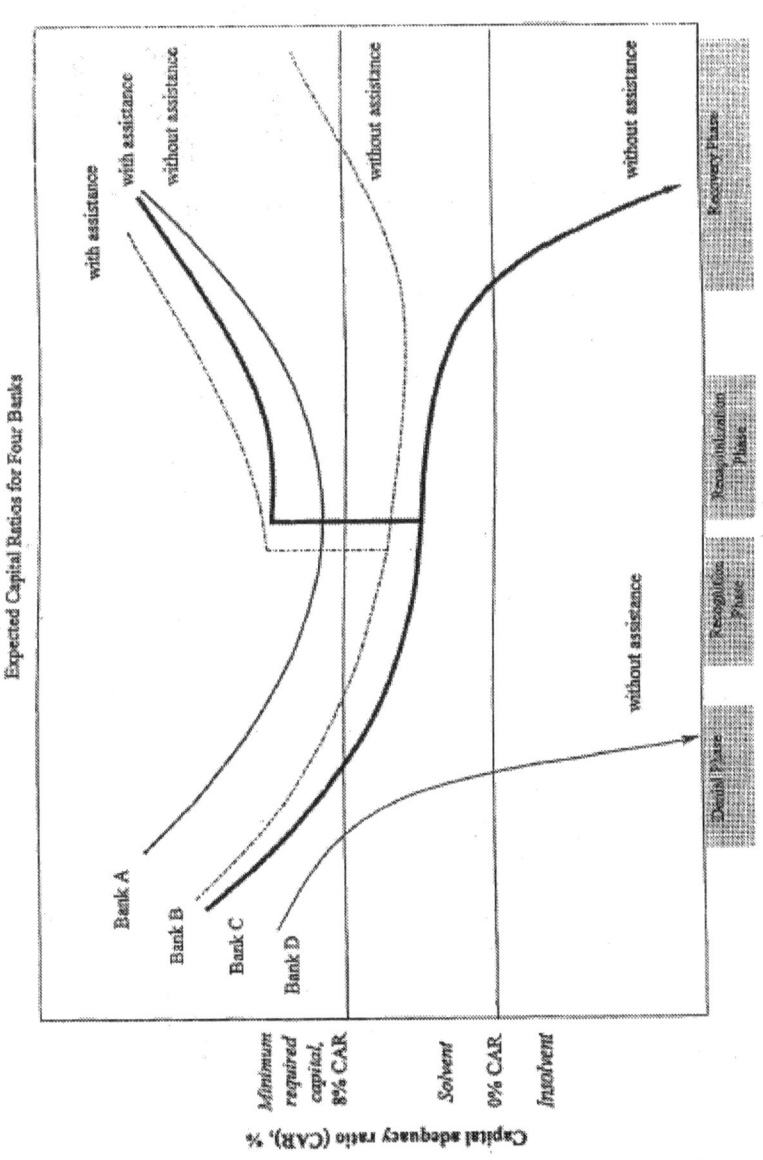

Expected Capital Ratios for Four Banks

Source: Adapted from "Loan Loss Recoveries and Debt Resolution Agencies: The Swedish Experience", S. Ingves and G. Lind, 1997.

13

struggle between sub-solvency and the minimum 8% CAR. Even banks claiming a CAR of 8% or greater do not always factor in the quality of their assets. For example a bank that claims a 10% CAR but has undisclosed asset losses of 30% actually has a CAR of negative 20%.[14] Thus, while the IMF CAR-curves may provide useful insight into establishing relative recapitalization targets, governments in transition economies are likely to see *real* downward pressure on all of the trajectories, as well as find it difficult to distinguish between categories (B), (C), and (D). There will also be very few banks in (A), since 'crisis management starts only after a substantial part of the banking sector has deteriorated [into the other categories].'[15] Chapter 4 highlights some of the complexities that Hungary experienced once bad loans were hived off into the state-owned Hungarian Investment and Development Corporation.

2.2.2   Conditionality

State involvement in a banking crisis is demonstrably essential. But funding is just one variable; the strings attached to the financing are the ultimate determinants of success. Behavioral and structural change must be induced. Perhaps one of the greatest challenges facing governments is how to provide financial resources without promulgating soft budget constraints. There tends to be a domino effect with this type of behavior. Unconditional recapitalization by the state leaves banks' management with little incentive to actively pursue bad loans because future bailouts are expected. Without pressure from the banks, enterprises become lax in servicing their loans.[16] In a speech before the IMF and World Bank on the dangers of unconditional bailouts, Leszek Balcerowicz warned that 'while working on the containment of the present problems, one should not weaken and complicate the defenses against future ones.'[17] The caveat against the knock-on effect is clear.

A 1995 study by Berglof and Roland demonstrated that banks might proactively engage in 'gambles for bailouts' behavior. In their model, banks did not have a financial incentive to refinance bad loans *ex post*. They instead chose to take advantage the government's soft budget policy:

> Since the government has an interest *ex post* in keeping unprofitable firms afloat, banks could commit capital to such firms beyond their current liquidity in order to trigger a

government bailout. Such 'gambles for bailout' may indeed
be profitable for a bank that only pays part of the cost of
refinancing firms, the residual being covered by the liquidity
injection from the government…gambles for bailouts are more
likely when loan portfolios are poor and banks
undercapitalized.[18]

Similar to problems with insurance, soft budget constraints and

the recapitalization of banks may lead to both *moral hazards* (lax

discipline) and *adverse selection* (benefiting from the up side of risky

investments, while protected on the down side).[19] Thus, the state must

utilize a combination of policies with recapitalization to engage hard

budget constraints.

The World Bank Report—1996 recognized recapitalization as a

wise use of the taxpayers' money only if it increases the strength of

the financial system and augments the potential for bank privatization.

Policies must focus on promoting 'self help' for banks to encourage

the build up of the capital base.[20] Interdependent policies that support

the government's (i.e., tax payers') recapitalization investment

include regulation, supervision and enforcement, enterprise

restructuring, bankruptcy, and privatization.

2.3   Regulation, supervision and enforcement

Without prudential regulation, supervision and enforcement, transition banking becomes a black hole for pecuniary state resources. From 1991 through 1993 Poland and Hungary established various forms of the following regulations to instill financial discipline into their banking systems: new loan classification schemes, mandatory loan provisioning measures, implementation of international accounting standards (IAS), Basle Committee capital standards, minimum capital requirements for new banks, exposure rules on solvency and deposit insurance.[21] Regulatory agencies were also established to implement these new regulations. In Poland, the responsibility fell under the Central Bank (National Bank of Poland), while Hungary opted for a separate government agency (the State Banking Supervisory Agency—SBSA). All of this looked good on paper. In reality, the regulatory organizations suffered from inexperience and difficult procedures for off-site and on-site inspections. With technical support from organizations such as the EBRD these agencies improved over time.[22]

An EBRD working paper emphasized that 'the [transition] banking system never will become strong if the supervisory arrangements do not seek to reflect the highest international standards from the earliest stage.'[23]   But even the EBRD was forced to recognize that the early stages of transition banking involve compromise.   Banks often had trouble complying with the new regulations because of the inherently unstable system.   Forcing do-or-die standards would almost certainly have led to a critical number of bank closures, potentially touching off an accelerated crisis.   The other end of the spectrum was regulatory forbearance.

Too much leniency would have facilitated the hazards of soft budget constraints, leading precisely to the problems that the regulations were intended to rectify.   Most transition countries thus attempted to phase in the regulations and enforcement over a period of time.   Evidence indicates that both Poland and Hungary started moving towards *relatively* better bank lending standards by 1993.[24]

Behavior modification has been a recurring theme in this section. 'Banking supervision may appear to be about numbers and ratios but it is essentially and fundamentally about people.'[25]   Decisions made by managers, directors and owners of banks must be objectively governed by enforced regulations. Hard budget constraints in the regulatory arena are ultimately necessary, but not sufficient, for the successful recapitalization of banks. Soft budget constrains, conversely, cause serious inefficiency.

2.4 Enterprise restructuring and bankruptcy

2.4.1 Enterprise restructuring: banks' interests

Enterprise restructuring is one of the primary objectives of microeconomic reform. It also plays a vital role to a bank's bottom line, since the health of enterprises ultimately affects the ability to service their loans. Early in the transition, the governments of Poland and Hungary made critical policy decisions on how to optimally address enterprise restructuring. The issue centered on bank-led versus government-led approaches. Chapters 3 and 4 show that Poland predominantly opted for the former, while part of Hungary's strategy included aspects of the latter, under the direction of the State Development and Investment Company.

James C. Mitchell, Jr.

There are two schools of thought on bank-led enterprise restructuring. Advocates argue that (a) other than the firm's managers, banks are likely to have more knowledge than anyone else on inside financial and credit information, and (b) use of this information can drive greater structural change in an enterprise; vis-à-vis government-influenced organizations, which have a propensity toward delay and obstruction.[26] Detractors argue that banks are not in a position, because of time and resources, to restructure both customers and themselves.

Another argument is based on the use of debt-equity swaps. Those advocating the procedure claim that a bank's solvency improves because ownership rights are exchanged for the bad debts. Thus, as a co-owner, the bank is key player in restructuring the firm. Critics maintain that '...when a banker has participation in the capital of a borrower company, it will find itself under strong pressure to increase the volume of loans to that borrower, even if the situation of the latter remains as difficult or worse than before.'[27] The caveats and concerns against bank-led restructuring are valid issues. Unfortunately, governments are also hamstrung with many of the same problems, and even more so, as the lessons from Hungary's partially centralized approach will bear out.

2.4.2   Bankruptcy policies

In theory, bankruptcy can lead to the reorganization of an enterprise and positively influence loan servicing. In practice, there is a liquidation bias built into most bankruptcy laws even in most advanced market economies. For example, the Chapter 11 procedure in the United States ultimately leads to liquidation in more than 90% of the cases.[28] The danger in implementing a hard-budget-constraint oriented bankruptcy program in transition economies is that most enterprises emerging from the 'soft' era of socialism would collapse, sending the number of bad loans held by the banks skyrocketing. However, the disciplining effects of bankruptcy laws, if structured properly, serve an important role in influencing the positive behavior of firms.

The concept of formal bankruptcy did not exit under socialism. When constructing bankruptcy laws, Stiglitz warns that importing a system designed for a developed market economy is particularly dangerous. Independent and competent judiciaries, the ability to physically handle the sheer number of cases and a weak culture for the development and restructuring of new businesses are some of the realistic workability issues to consider.[29] In an ironic twist, Poland's financial distress policies were arguably soft (but creative); Hungary conversely adopted very stringent bankruptcy codes early in the transition. The impacts on the bad loan problem, as outlined in the following chapters, were almost predictable.

2.5   Privatization

If properly undertaken, recapitalization and privatization are complementary. Banks must have the correct inducements to make prudent decisions. This paper plainly illustrated the malfeasance that arises from inappropriate incentive structures. One of the potential benefits of the privatization of commercial banks is the positive influence on all levels of management. The caveat applicable to enterprise privatization, however, also applies to banks: privatization may be necessary, but it is not sufficient, to promote economic efficiency. A framework of effective laws and regulations is necessary to underpin successful privatization. The banking crisis in Chile serves as an excellent example of the disastrous consequences of unregulated privatization. The EBRD correctly warns that 'the privatization of commercial banks should proceed cautiously, if at all, as long as effective regulatory mechanisms are not in place.'[30] The trade off with the status quo, however, is also controversial. Until banks are privatized, there will continue to be pressure by the state on bank's lending decisions.

In addition to complementarity, bank recapitalization and privatization are also paradoxical. 'Bank privatization may be necessary to avoid the re-appearance of bad loans, but the resolution of the bad loans problem is necessary for privatization.'[31] The rate of bank privatization proceeded slowly in both Poland and Hungary. By 1994, only three of fourteen state-owned regional commercial banks were privatized in Poland, while there were none in Hungary. These statistics, in part, reflect the impact of both recapitalization and associated policies on privatization efficiency. Chapters 3 and 4 comparatively link the resolution of the bad loan problem to privatization.

James C. Mitchell, Jr.

Notes

1 Leszek Balcerowicz: *Socialism Capitalism Transformation*. Budapest: Central European Press, 1995, p.224.
2 Dariusz K. Rosati: The Polish Experience. In Steven Fries: Transition: private sector development and the role of financial institutions. EBRD Working Paper No.13, July 1994, p.20.
3 Istvan Abel and John P. Bonin: Financial Sector Reform in the Economies in Transition: On the Way to Privatizing Commercial Banks. In Bonin & Szekely, *The Development and Reform of Financial Systems in Central and Eastern Europe*. England: Edward Elgar Publishing Limited, 1994, p.116.
4 Peter Dittus: Bank reform and behavior in Central Europe. *Journal of Comparative economics* 19: p.343.
5 David Begg and Richard Portes: Enterprise debt and economic transformation: financial restructuring in Central and Eastern Europe. In Mayer & Vives: *Capital markets and financial institutions*. Cambridge: Cambridge University Press, 1992, p.237.
6 Eva Varhegyi: The 'Second' Reform of the Hungarian Banking System. In Bonin & Szekely, 1994, p.293.
7 Ronald W. Anderson and Chantal Kegels: *Transition Banking, Financial Development of Central and Eastern Europe*. United States: Oxford University Press Inc., 1998, p.23.
8 IBID.
9 Leszek Balcerowicz: speech before the International Monetary Fund and World Bank Group Board of Governors Annual Meeting. Washington, D.C., October 6-8, 1998, p.1.
10 Charles Enoch, Gillian Garcia and V. Sundararajan: Recapitalizing Banks with Public Funds: Selected Issues. IMF Working Paper WP/99/139, 1999, p.46. Note: 'The Basle Capital Accord assigns risk-weights to on- and off-balance sheet exposures, according to broad categories of relative riskiness. The Accord sets minimum capital ratio requirements...(at) 8 percent for total capital in relation to risk-weighted assets.'
11 IBID., p.17.
12 IBID.
13 IBID. (Graph reproduction, p.18.)

14 Aristobulo de Juan: "False Friends" in Banking Reform. In Steven Fries: Building sound banking in transition economies. EBRD Working Paper No. 17, April 1996, p.38.

15 Enoch, et al: IMF Working Paper WP/99/139, 1999, p.19.

16 European Bank for Reconstruction and Development: *Transition report 1997—Enterprise performance and growth.* United Kingdom: EBRD Publications, 1997, p.85.

17 Leszek Balcerowicz: IMF WB speech. 1998, p.2.

18 Erik Berglof and Gerard Roland: Bank Restructuring and Soft Budget Constraints in Financial Transition. London: Centre for Economic Policy Research. Discussion Paper No. 1250 (November 1995), p.1.

19 Willem H. Buiter, Ricardo Lago and Helen Rey: Financing transition: investing in enterprises during macroeconomic transition. EBRD Working Paper No. 35, December 1998, p.7.

20 The World Bank: *World Development Report 1996—From Plan to Market.* New York: Oxford University Press. 1996, p.103.

21 Peter Dittus: Bank Reform and Behavior in Central Europe. pp.344-345.

22 IBID.

23 Brian Quinn: Banking Supervision in the Transition Economy. EBRD Working Paper No.17 (1996), p.25.

24 Peter Dittus: Bank Reform and Behavior in Central Europe. p.346. Note: Measured by net enterprise borrowing from domestic banks, as a percentage of net interest due.

25 Brian Quinn: Banking Supervision in the Transition Economy. p.25.

26 Sweder van Wijnbergen: Bank restructuring and enterprise reform. EBRD Working Paper No.29 (1998), p.26.

27 Dr. Martin Raiser, Principal Economist—EBRD, private interview on 28 July 2000 in London, England. Quote from: Aristobulo du Juan: "False Friends" in Banking Reform. p.43.

28 Sweder van Wijnbergen: Bank restructuring and enterprise reform. p.1.

29 Joseph Stiglitz: Whither Reform? Ten Years of the Transition. Keynote Address: World Bank Annual Bank Conference on Development Economics. Washington, D.C. (April 1999), p.7.

30 Sweder van Wijnbergen: Bank restructuring and enterprise reform. p.10.

31 Jacek Rostowski: *Banking Reform in Central and Eastern Europe and the Former Soviet Union.* Budapest: Central European University Press, 1995, p.8.

Chapter 3

Poland

3.1   Organization and approach

Poland did not take a uniform approach to banks' bad loan problems and recapitalization.   Understanding the advantages and constraints of the Polish strategy therefore requires an organizational knowledge of the banking system.   In addition to the monobank, Narodowy Bank Polski (National Bank of Poland—NBP), a few specialized state-owned banks existed.   The Banking Law of 1989 split the NBP into a two-tiered structure.   Subsequent amendments allowed for the development of joint stock companies (JSCs). Although significant in number, approximately 78 by 1992,[1] most JSCs were generally small and undercapitalized.   Concentrated amongst 15 banks, the specialized and regional state banks dominated the lion's share of the industry.

Table 3.1
Distribution of bank assets in Poland (million Zlotys)

	Dec. 1992	%T
Specialized state banks	337,886,000	52%
Regional state banks	191,397,000	29%
Others	123,427,000	19%
Total	652,710,000	

Source: Anderson & Kegels (1998)[2]

Table 3.1 indicates the dominance of state ownership in the Polish banking system. Recall from Chapter 2 that many JSCs were directly or indirectly owned by the state; and government involvement in banking was even more overwhelming.

The strengths and weaknesses of the Polish recapitalization program may be analyzed by disaggregating the specialized and regional state banks. Chart 3.1 orders the 15 largest banks according to their 1993 assets.[3] The nine regional commercial banks were split off from the NBP. Part of their baggage included both poor and non-performing loans. The specialized state banks also had deeply problematical loan portfolios. Their difficulties were even more complex than the regional commercial banks'. Specialized banks were both big and politically charged. For example, PKO-BP was the largest commercial bank and the state savings bank. BGZ specialized in agriculture, a major sector of the Polish economy. Similar to other large banks, the treasury predominantly owned BGZ and PKO-BP. BGZ, however, was also the 'big brother' to about 1,600 rural cooperative banks. The relationship was reflected in the large minority ownership (46%) of these organizations. 'This interlocking control structure has arguably been the origin of the considerable problems with bad loans in the agricultural sector and has impeded the restructuring at BGZ.'[4] When the former Prime Minister of Poland, Jan Krzysztof Bielecki, was asked why the restructuring of BGZ had been such a failure, in light of Poland's other successes, he alluded to the ownership problem and political influence, even questioning the definition of BGZ as a 'bank.' Mr. Bielecki rather compared it to 'a lot of local cashiers.'[5] With political issues influencing the specialized banks, the success story associated with the Polish banking reforms was essentially limited to the regional commercial bank sector.

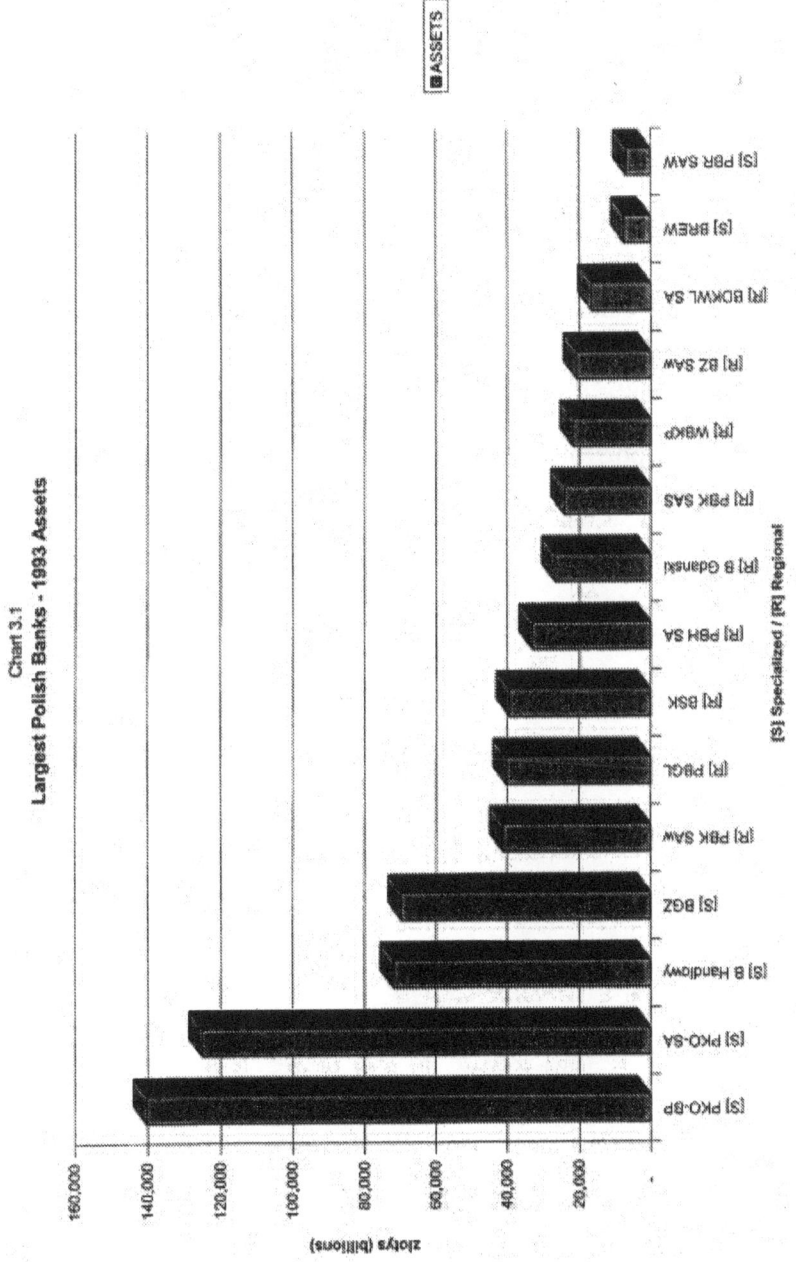

Chart 3.1
Largest Polish Banks - 1993 Assets

Not surprisingly, the loans of emerging new private banks were oriented towards private enterprises. By 1994 these loans comprised 72% of their portfolios. The opposite was true for the spun-off regional banks. As part of the inheritance, 60% of their lending was geared towards state-owned enterprises. An interesting statistic was the orientation of specialized banks that leant to private enterprises (52% of their portfolios). BGZ's 82% lending to the agricultural sector, which was privatized, skewed the high percentage.[6] Lending to the private sector, versus SOEs, was therefore no guarantee against politically oriented bad loans. This situation became more untenable with the influence of the Communist and Peasant Parties by 1994 and 1995.[7]

The focus of Polish bank reform centered on cleaning up the stock and flow problems of the SOE-oriented regional commercial banks. With bad loans escalating, Prime Minister Bielecki found himself in a banking crisis that had been played out elsewhere in the world; only this time, the entire micro and macro economy were struggling on the brink of instability. Complicating matters further, the Polish Minister of Finance, Leszek Balcerowicz, was unavailable due to personal reasons. In consultation with three former Finance Ministers from Spain, Portugal and Chile, the Polish Deputy Minister of Finance (Kawalec), and the International Finance Corporation (Karfenburger), Mr. Bielecki pulled the trigger on a decentralized, once-off strategy.[8] The former Finance Ministers provided excellent guidance, as they had witnessed the pitfalls of government-led schemes first hand.

With the strategy set, the next issue hinged on funding. Chapter 2 illustrated the severe fiscal problems facing transition governments. But Poland had, with G24 assistance, smartly 'kept dollars under the mattress'. The total was four to five billion U.S. dollars. A stabilization fund was established on the eve of Polish reforms. Approximately one billion dollars were allocated for the sustainability of the currency exchange. After two to three years, with the exchange rate mechanism in place, there was no need for the fund; the zloty was convertible. About 60% of the currency exchange fund was then reallocated for the protection of government bonds, to be used for bank recapitalization.[9] A sound plan and funding were now both in-place to address the banking crisis.

3.2   1993 law on financial restructuring

Before the implementation of the Law on Financial Restructuring of Enterprises and Banks in February 1993, the Ministry of Finance took important precursor steps in 1991 and 1992 to prepare banks for their new responsibilities. The nine state-owned regional commercial banks were mandated to: 1) establish debt workout departments and assign bad debts to them, 2) preclude borrowers with loans classified as doubtful or unrecoverable from receiving further credit, and 3) initiate a review process and develop action plans for all delinquent customers.[10] By the time the 1993 financial restructuring law was enacted, banks were already getting acclimated to operating in a decentralized, incentive-based environment. The 1993 law built on this foundation.   The general objectives of the law were to 'rehabilitate the financial sector of the economy [commercial banks], to allow good state enterprises to restructure and eventually expand, and to eliminate permanent loss-makers.'[11]   A conditional link to receiving the one-time recapitalization funds was restructuring the debt.

The strength of the Polish strategy rested on a new restructuring procedure, bank conciliation. Prior to this course of action, enterprises under severe financial duress had three relatively difficult options: liquidation, bankruptcy or court conciliation. Bank conciliation provided a more efficient alternative. The key modifications were:

> (i) an agreement to restructure the liabilities required the approval of at least 50 percent of the creditors by value (as opposed to 80 percent under court conciliation), (ii) tax liabilities were included which meant for debtors with large tax arrears a restructuring plan was readily accepted once it has government approval, and (iii) if a secured debtor refused to participate in conciliation his claim was limited to his security…[it also] permits creditors to accept either new debt or equity or both in exchange for writing off old loans.[12]

In tandem with the bank-led work out program, the government issued bonds (valued at 11 trillion zlotys) to the nine regional commercial banks free-of-charge. The targeted CAR was set at 12%. Other banks received treasury bonds (valued at 10 trillion zlotys) at market-based interest rates. To qualify for the funds, the regional banks had to restructure the SOE loans that were outstanding by the

end of 1991. Restructuring also had to be completed within one year.
If no agreement was reached between the bank and the enterprise, the
bank had to initiate formal bankruptcy procedures or sell the bad
asset.[13]   While the Polish strategy had internal flexibility for
negotiations, external incentives and constraints were established for
both parties to resolve the bad loan problem.

3.3   Results

Table 3.2
1993 Financial Restructuring Law
[For seven regional commercial banks]

Total loans qualified	792
Value (million zlotys)	15,748,795
Credit Classification	Percentage
Non-performing	14
Substandard	8
Doubtful	8
Loss	62
Unclassified	8
Value of loans processed	15,687,809
Distribution by method	Percentage
Bank conciliation	48
Loan sales	6
Liquidation	3
Bankruptcy	10
Paid in full	11
Renewed servicing	22

Source: Anderson & Kegels (1998)[14]

One of the important achievements of the 1993 Polish law is that it effectively altered behavior and drove change. An independent study undertaken by Gray and Holle (1996) indicated that the law was a factor in causing passive creditors to take action against bad debtors. They point to the fact that most of the marked debts had gone bad by 1991, but creditors took no action in almost 80% of their sample cases until the law was passed in 1993. While the restructuring of debt was achieved, very few firms were actually restructured. In particular, debt-equity swaps were not used as widely as expected (2% of the cases). One of the reasons may have been the very short time frame given to resolve the bad debt problem.[15]

The impact of the law on the targeted regional banks was striking, vis-à-vis the specialized banks, which were not ultimately covered by it. Political issues (e.g., agriculture and savings) affected the specialized banks' non-involvement.[16] The law covered seven of the regional commercial banks. Two others were recapitalized independently as part of their privatization. Table 3.2 indicates that bank conciliation was a preferred method of restructuring bad loans, especially given the difficulties outlined in Chapter 2 concerning bankruptcy and liquidation. Another positive outcome was the relatively high number of loans that returned to regular servicing or were paid off (over one-third).[17]   The previously established, interdependent criteria for a successful recapitalization policy were solving the bad loan problem on a once-off basis and increasing the capitalization rate. The Polish law achieved both of these objectives. By the end of 1994, the seven regional banks had CARs in excess of 20%, well beyond the 12% target; and the problem loans that were covered by the restructuring have not re-emerged.[18]   Moreover, the EBRD reports that most of these banks are now private. And what about the politically charged, specialized state-owned banks not covered by the law?   The representative statistics[19] speak for themselves:

PKO-BP →   1990-1992: operating losses of 29 trillion zlotys covered by the state

1994: 20% bad loan problem

1994: recapitalized with 6 trillion zlotys of treasury bonds

1994-1995: deposit growth despite bad performance; 'state protected'

1999: state-owned

BGZ   →   1994: 45% bad loan problem

1994: recapitalized with 12 trillion zlotys

1994: additional 13 trillion zlotys needed to raise CAR to 8%

1999: state-owned

Notes

1 Ronald W. Anderson and Chantal Kegels: *Transition Banking, Financial Development of Central and Eastern Europe.* United States: Oxford University Press Inc., 1998, pp.133-134. Note: 87 commercial banks minus the 9 regional banks. This number excludes the approximately 1,600 agricultural cooperative banks and foreign banks.
2 IBID.
3 IBID., p.136.
4 IBID., p.135.
5 Jan Krzysztof Bielecki, former Prime Minister of Poland—1991, private interview on 28 July 2000 in London, England.
6 Ronald W. Anderson and Chantal Kegels: *Transition Banking.* p.149.
7 Jan Krzysztof Bielecki private interview on 28 July 2000.
8 IBID.
9 IBID.
10 Peter Dittus: Bank reform and behavior in Central Europe. *Journal of Comparative economics* 19: p.340.
11 Dariusz K. Rosati: The Polish Experience. In Steven Fries: Transition: private sector development and the role of financial institutions. EBRD Working Paper No.13, July 1994, p.24.
12 Ronald W. Anderson and Chantal Kegels: *Transition Banking.* p.162.
13 Peter Dittus: Bank Reform and Behavior in Central Europe. p.341.
14 Ronald W. Anderson and Chantal Kegels: *Transition Banking.* p.163.
15 Cheryl W. Gray and Arnold Holle: Bank-led restructuring in Poland: the conciliation process in action. *Economics of Transition*, Volume 4 (2), 1996, pp.365-366.
16 Jan Krzysztof Bielecki private interview on 28 July 2000.
17 Ronald W. Anderson and Chantal Kegels: *Transition Banking.* p.164.
18 Sweder van Wijnbergen: Bank restructuring and enterprise reform. EBRD Working Paper No.29 (1998), p.15.
19 Ronald W. Anderson and Chantal Kegels: *Transition Banking.* pp.164-165.

Chapter 4

Hungary

4.1   Antecedents and developments

4.1.1   Legacy

More so than many of its CEE counterparts in the latter twentieth century, Hungary significantly departed from the Soviet economic model. In 1968 the New Economic Mechanism effectively eliminated quantitative planning and emphasized decentralization. Despite the apparent radical direction of the Hungarian economy an insidious aspect of socialism doggedly persisted, namely soft budget constraints. Enterprises remained firmly entrenched in government's pocket for soft loans and subsidies. This fact is not meant to insinuate that developed market economies do not practice various forms of subsidization. But in Hungary, there was a continued mindset of expectation. Furthermore, many of the economy's most productive assets were still owned or controlled by the state. Therefore, while decision-making power devolved, the state remained a very important and influential actor: Hungarian government expenditures in the late 1980s were approximately 64% of GNP, versus 46% and 37% in West Germany and the United States, respectively.[1]

The legacy of Hungarian market socialism uniquely dominated the post-collapse environment. 'A decision-maker's power was not necessarily derived from the party but rather from the fact that others could not mount an effective challenge against his position.'[2] The power of the decision-maker was therefore not fractured when communism collapsed. Anderson and Kegels (1999) formulated that this dynamic led to a lack of legitimate consensus on radically restructuring many of Hungary's institutions. It was also keenly reflected in the incremental approach taken to reforming the banking sector.

4.1.2 Evolution and structure

After a lapse of almost 40 years, Hungary returned to a two-tiered banking system on 1 January 1987. The commercial banks that were established primarily drew their branch offices and clients from the National Bank of Hungary (NBH).[3] From 1987 until 1991 the number of commercial banks more than doubled, from 15 to 32. While this statistic accounts for the growth of newly established private banks, it masks the continued dominance of state ownership. Table 4.1 disaggregates banks' ownership structures and accentuates the prevalence of state involvement. It includes both direct and indirect (i.e., through SOEs) ownership by the state.

Table 4.1
Share of state ownership in the Hungarian banking sector
by the end of 1991

Group of Banks	Share capital (HUF* mn)	Direct state ownership %	Indirect state ownership %	Total state ownership %
National Savings and Commercial Bank	23,000	100.0	0.0	100.0
Large commercial banks**	43,093	44.2	30.7	74.9
Mid-sized banks	36,343	3.7	36.8	40.5
Total	117,172	38.0	28.0	66.0

* Hungarian Forint
** Hungarian Credit Bank, Commercial and Credit Bank, Hungarian Foreign Trade Bank, Budapest Bank

Source: Eva Varhegyi (1994)[4]

The government substantially controlled the capital shares of the five largest banks. Harms from state dominance in the banking sector and the benefits of correctly implemented privatization were highlighted in previous chapters. Very early in the transition (before 1991), two issues particularly affected financial efficiency in Hungary. First, the state was initially more interested in maximizing tax receipts from banks than recognizing or addressing banks' bad loan predicament. Second, the government was predisposed to viewing banks' credit policies as the primary problem in the economy, rather than tackle the more fundamental, inherent difficulties in the marketplace (e.g., decline of national industries and agriculture).[5] These factors, combined with the problem of cross-ownership lending bias, contributed to the inefficient allocation of capital. State-ownership obstacles endured through the early and mid 1990s, as evidenced by only one commercial bank being partially privatized by late 1994.

4.1.3 Laws, institutions and bankruptcy

The importance of establishing effective laws, regulations and institutions were a prime focus of Chapter 2. It was underscored by the impact on bank supervision and behavior modification. Hungary took substantial measures in the 1991 to create a financial framework in-line with the developed European market economies. The Act on the National Bank of Hungary [No. LX], the Act on Financial Institutions and Financial Institutional Activities [No. LXIX] and the New Banking Act were instrumental in protecting banks from political influence and implementing discipline in the financial system. Critical objectives of the latter two measures included raising banks' CARs to 8% by the end of 1994 and the classification of non-performing loans (doubtful, substandard and bad), with mandated provisions varying from 20 to 100 percent. Banks were also limited on their risk exposure to large customers. Additionally, The Act on Accounting [No. XLIII] established adequate reserves against doubtful claims.[6] While these well-conceived laws and regulations provided an essential foundation for the financial system, the EBRD noted that the early years suffered from implementation problems (under the State Banking Supervision Agency—SBSA and the NBH), precisely for the reasons outlined in Chapter 2 (e.g., supervision, monitoring, enforcement, etc.).[7]

The Hungarian government became increasingly concerned about the growth of creditor passivity. Existing bankruptcy laws did not provide an incentive for creditors or debtors to take any substantial action. There were only about 1,000 bankruptcy filings (50 involving SOEs) between 1986 and 1991. With a low level of loss provision and capital, the banks were essentially unable to initiate bankruptcy procedures against large SOEs, their main customers.[8] That changed on 1 January 1992 when Hungary enacted the New Bankruptcy Law. In an effort to initiate enterprise restructuring and enforce hard budget constraints, the law required a firm with any outstanding debt greater than 90 days to file for bankruptcy. The penalty for noncompliance was a criminal offence. The impact was felt almost immediately. By the end of 1992 bankruptcy and liquidation filings skyrocketed to 4,169 and 9,891, respectively. The system was virtually overwhelmed, as highlighted by the actual number of cases closed: bankruptcy (2,703) and liquidations (4,936).[9] The New Bankruptcy

Law was amended and tweaked multiple times in the early 1990s to mollify the drastic impact on the economy. While the economic complexity of the law is beyond the scope of this paper, its direct impact on banks' bottom-lines was significant. Taken in tandem with the New Banking Act (categorizing and provisioning of loans), banks were pushed into a solvency crisis.

> By the end of 1992, the aggregate stock of qualified loans stood at HUF 262 bn which amounted to 17.2 per cent of the total loan portfolio and about 10 per cent of GDP. Full statutory provisions for the banking system increased from HUF 83 bn to HUF 222.5 bn from 1991 to 1992, an increment that exceeds the 1992 profits *before* tax and provisions by almost 300 per cent. Total equity and provisions of the banking system amounted to HUF 267.9 bn at the end of December 1992.[10]

4.2 The loan consolidation schemes

Hungary adopted some of Central and Eastern Europe's most stringent laws and regulations. It also used a decentralized (creditor-negotiated) approach to restructuring enterprises. Yet these efforts were seriously undermined when Hungary took the opposite tactic for managing bad loans and bank recapitalizations. When the new banking and bankruptcy laws caused non-performing loans to surge to

11% of GDP by the end of 1992, the state responded with a series of

credit consolidation schemes. Loans classified as 'lost' were moved

off banks' books and swapped with 20-year bonds (14 strategic SOEs

were targeted for special government support). 'Lost' loans were then

transferred to a government recovery agency, the Hungarian

Investment and Development Corporation (MBFRt).[11] One problem

was that other non-performing loans remained with the banks. The

same enterprises could therefore have loans in both places. 'This

complicated the recovery agency's job and gave incentives to banks

once again to engage in cosmetic cover-ups through lending simply to

prevent more loans from showing up as bad.'[12] Moreover, the

MBFRt did not have a clear mandate for recovering the bad loans.

They also lacked managerial experience and had a limited knowledge

about the borrowers. The insufficient staff (eighty people to manage

1,885 borrowers) actually had to ask the banks to continue to manage

the carved-out loans until the middle of 1993.[13] While the capital

injection temporarily improved banks' CARs, the lack of attention to

effectively managing the bad loan problem eventually boomeranged.

By 1993 the percentage of non-performing assets (NPA) jumped to

James C. Mitchell, Jr.

15.7%, up from 7.5% in 1992. Another recapitalization was required in 1993, eventually drawing the NPA percentage down to 11% in 1994. The 1993 approach, however, had a different spin. The state did not buy the debt. A two-stage strategy was developed whereby banks received capital from the government and then worked out the loans themselves. The Ministry of Finance thus became an even more dominant shareholder in the large commercial banks.[14] This approach could best be described as quasi-decentralized. 'The conservative-nationalist government seemed determined to learn the lesson of the "trap of centralization" from its own experience.'[15] The state, however, appears to have walked into another trap, described earlier by Berglof and Roland as 'gambles for bailouts.' Banks had responsibility for the loans on their books, but their owners had deep, soft pockets. Worse yet, the state proved to be a very poor monitor of the recapitalization funds. Even after the 1993 scheme, five of the eight primary banks in the program still had negatives CARs. Unsurprisingly, this promulgated further bailouts, despite repeated warnings by the government to the contrary. Table 4.2 illustrates the financial ramifications of Hungary's recapitalization strategy.

46

Table 4.2
Hungarian bailouts: itemized impact

Date	Name	Amount (Forint billions)	Intervention
Summer 1991		10.5	- State guarantee
1992	Loan consolidation	80.0	- Bad loans swapped for consolidation bonds. Bad loans transferred to MBFRt, state-owned financial institution.
July 1992	Clean-up of bank's portfolios program	57.0	- Consolidation bonds
April 1993	First stage of bank recapitalization program	114.0	- Consolidation bonds
		1.9	- Purchase of shares from SOEs
		5.0	- Subordinated debt in the form of consolidation bonds
		8.6	- New shares acquired against consolidation bonds
May 1994	First round of the second stage of bank recapitalization program	18.0	- Consolidation bonds
December 1994	Last round of the second stage of bank recapitalization program	15.0	- Consolidation bonds

Source: Anderson & Kegels (1998) [16]

The Hungarian solution to the bad loan dilemma obviously did not solve the flow problem. Since the state focused more on debt relief, both enterprises and debts failed to undergo fundamental restructuring. Another serious problem was the low level of recapitalization. The entire banking system looked relatively healthy at an 11% CAR in 1993 (caveat on asset quality). However, the early threshold for key targeted banks, set at 8%, was later revised to 0%. Recall from the IMF objectives in figure 2.1, the recovery phase of all recapitalization plans exceeded the 8% threshold. Lowered CARs and continued credit pressure from SOEs kept banks in the position of taking risky loans. Worse yet, Backe (1994)[17] maintains that an insufficient degree of recapitalization (e.g., 0%) would not likely even solve the stock problem. 'In practice, the initial efforts were far too small to resolve the problem, so that in a short time [the government] found it had to intervene again.'[18] This firmly established the expectation for future bailouts. A fundamental lesson from the Hungarian experience is that insufficient recapitalization in the short-term can be very costly in the long-term. Sufficient recapitalization might not lead to hard budget constraints, but inadequate capital injections will probably drive soft budget constraints.

After spending over three billion dollars by the mid 1990s, what were the results of the Hungarian government's bank bailout and debt consolidation schemes?

- Failed restructuring of the banking system
- Failed restructuring of enterprises
- Failed incentive structures of banks and enterprises, except a reinforced dependency on the state[19]

The transition literature is generally harsh on the Hungary's centralized and soft approach to the management of liabilities. Once entangled in the process, the state found it very difficult to extricate itself. The perpetuated economic costs of the Hungarian policies have been clearly delineated. But were there political benefits? Mizsei (1995) noted that the broad and generous nature of the debtor consolidation scheme was clearly meant to serve the election prospects of the government.[20] Jan Krzysztof Bielecki, the former Prime Minister of Poland, also recognized the clear political advantages of the centralized approach.[21] Yet he opted not to open

James C. Mitchell, Jr.

the Pandora's Box. Despite the 'once-off' rhetoric, Hungary's

decision to pursue centralized management in a transition

environment was the first step towards the politics of soft budget

constraints.

Notes

1 Ronald W. Anderson and Chantal Kegels: *Transition Banking, Financial Development of Central and Eastern Europe.* United States: Oxford University Press Inc., 1998, p.74.
2 IBID., p.75.
3 www.mnb.hu/english/1_about/history.htm
4 Eva Varhegyi: The 'Second' Reform of the Hungarian Banking System. In Bonin & Szekely, *The Development and Reform of Financial Systems in Central and Eastern Europe.* England: Edward Elgar Publishing Limited, 1994, p.308.
5 IBID., p.297.
6 IBID., pp.294-295.
7 European Bank for Reconstruction and Development: *Transition report update. United Kingdom*: EBRD Publications, April 1999, pp.155-157.
8 Ronald W. Anderson and Chantal Kegels: *Transition Banking.* p.108.
9 IBID., p.110.
10 Istvan Abel and John P. Bonin: Financial Sector Reform in the Economies in Transition: On the Way to Privatizing Commercial Banks. In Bonin & Szekely, 1994, p.118.
11 www.mfb.hu Interpreted by G. Velisek, London School of Economics (July 2000).
12 Sweder van Wijnbergen: Bank restructuring and enterprise reform. EBRD Working Paper No.29 (1998), p.16.
13 Ronald W. Anderson and Chantal Kegels: *Transition Banking.* p.103.
14 David Stark and Laszlo Bruszt: *Post Socialist Pathways—Transforming Politics and Property in East Central Europe.* United Kingdom: Cambridge University Press, 1998, p.151.

15 IBID.
16 Ronald W. Anderson and Chantal Kegels: *Transition Banking.* p.102.
17 Peter Backe: Discussion on Eva Varhegyi's, The 'Second' Reform of the Hungarian Banking System. In Bonin & Szekely, 1994, p.311.
18 Ronald W. Anderson and Chantal Kegels: *Transition Banking.* p.129.
19 David Stark and Laszlo Bruszt: *Post Socialist Pathways—Transforming Politics and Property in East Central Europe.* p.152.
20 Kalman Mizsei: Lessons from Bad Management in the East Central European Economic Transition for the Second Wave of Reform Countries. In Jacek Rostowski: *Banking Reform in Central and Eastern Europe and the Former Soviet Union.* Budapest: Central European University Press, 1995, p.74.
21 Jan Krzysztof Bielecki, former Prime Minister of Poland—1991, private interview on 28 July 2000 in London, England.

James C. Mitchell, Jr.

Conclusion

'Communism should be regarded as "a fairy tale."'
Russian President, Vladimir Putin[1]

Unfortunately the *Alice in Wonderland* economic story did not end with the collapse of communism. In a transition environment probably best described as tsunami economics, a fundamentally flawed banking system emerged. Banks required that their ledgers be purged of bad loans and the assets recapitalized. This practice is not uncommon when developed market economies are involved in a severe banking crisis. In the CEE countries, however, the integral elements of a functional market economy were either missing or underdeveloped. Many of the bad loans were also made in a defunct system. Any assessment of a transition country's recapitalization strategy must therefore be underpinned by the interdependencies of financial conditionality, effective institutions, regulations and supervision, enterprise restructuring, privatization and bankruptcy policies. Too much strength or weakness in any one area may concomitantly lead to economic disequilibrium.

The transition literature broadly categorizes Poland's recapitalization strategy as successful, when compared with Hungary's approach. This paper generally agrees with the assessment but raises important caveats. Poland's strategy was not ubiquitous; the 1993 Law on Financial Restructuring of Enterprises and Banks only covered the regional commercial banks. Political issues precluded the large specialized banks from the hard budget constraints associated with the law. The high cost and multiple bailouts of PKO-BP and BGZ were telling signs of a failed aspect of the policy. The regional commercial banks, conversely, provided a brilliant example of efficient policy: bank-led (decentralized) debt workouts and hard budget constraints resolved the stock and flow problems.

Poland and Hungary entered the transition from different political and economic starting points. As a comparative common denominator, the primary determinant of a successful strategy was a permanent solution to the non-performing loans and a once-off recapitalization. This was precisely where Hungary failed. In 1992 the partially centralized approach entangled the state in a web of soft budget constraints. State-led centralized loan recovery may work in developed market economies, but the experience of Hungary indicates that transition governments may not have the expertise or resources to effectively manage the problem. When Hungary tried to move toward a bank-led resolution in 1993 it took a larger ownership share of the banks. The banks' deep-pocket mentality unfortunately became further entrenched. Additionally, a draconian bankruptcy law intended to induce enterprise reorganization had the effect of ballooning bad loans. These issues, combined with insufficient capital injections, promulgated multiple recapitalizations and recurrent non-performing loans.

The legitimate and efficacious privatization of state-owned banks is a good indicator of a successful recapitalization program. In addition to increased financial efficiency, a healthy bank may be sold by the state and enrich the government's coffers. That is why former Polish Prime Minister Jan Krzysztof Bielecki reinforced bank recapitalization and privatization as inseparable.[2] Using this criterion, Poland's 1993 Law on Financial Restructuring of Enterprises and Banks was a success. Almost all of the regional commercial banks in Poland are now privatized. Poland's specialized banks, however, and some of Hungary's large commercial banks are still in the hands of the state.[3]

The linkage between the micro and macro economy is essential to fledgling economic reforms in transition economies. Successful stabilization policies and price liberalization are dependent on a sound financial system. A crisis in the banking sector can thus facilitate an economic collapse. Moreover, 'only solvent banks—subject themselves to hard budget constraints *ex-ante* and *ex-post*—can be expected to impose a hard budget constraint on others.'[4] Government intervention must therefore be efficient and effective. The state will have to pay a price to stabilize the banking sector: the question is *how much*. The price tag is ultimately determined by the success of the bad loan and recapitalization policies. Transition economies are fundamentally unstable. Worse yet, the prevailing mindset is inherently linked to a past that was centrally state-dominated and ripe with soft budget constraints. Governments must therefore strongly evaluate both the economic and political ramifications of state policies. Winston Churchill said that sometimes one has to look back to move forward: a lesson that buoyed Poland's policy on regional commercial banks. Individuals with the best available information made decisions under incentive-based conditions. George Santayana would have better described Hungary's recapitalization policy and Poland's approach to the specialized banks: those who cannot remember the past are condemned to repeat it.

Notes

1 *George* magazine, Volume V Number 7, August 2000, p.98.
2 Jan Krzysztof Bielecki, former Prime Minister of Poland—1991, private interview on 28 July 2000 in London, England.
3 European Bank for Reconstruction and Development: *Transition report— Financial sector in transition.* United Kingdom: EBRD Publications, 1998, p.171 and p.183. Note: The asset share of state-owned banks generally declined in both countries by the late 1990s.
4 Ricardo Lago: Macroeconomic Stabilization, Systemic Transformation and Bank Solvency. In Steven Fries: Building sound banking in transition economies. EBRD Working Paper No. 17, April 1996, p.13.

James C. Mitchell, Jr.

Bibliography

Primary Material

A. Unpublished
1. Bielecki, Jan Krzysztof, former Primer Minister of Poland - 1991, private interview on 28 July 2000 in London, England.
2. Krkoska, Libor, Economist - European Bank for Reconstruction and Development, private interview on 28 July 2000 in London, England.
3. Raiser, Dr. Martin, Principal Economist - European Bank for Reconstruction and Development, private interview on 28 July 2000 in London, England.
4. http://www.mfb.hu/english/8index.htm
5. http://www.mfb.hu/english/1_about/oper.htm
6. http://www.mfb.hu/ [interpreted by G. Velisek - London School of Economics]
7. http://www.mnb.hu/english
8. http://www.nbp.pl.en/onbp/historia.html
9. http://www.pszaf.hu/english
10. http://www.otpbank.hu/online/english/f3

B. Published
1. Act LX of 1991 on The National Bank of Hungary (www.mnb.hu/english)
2. Balcerowicz, Leszek: speech before the International Monetary Fund and World Bank Group Board of Governors Annual Meeting. Washington, D.C., October 6 - 8, 1998. Press Release No. 23
3. Stiglitz, Joseph: Whither Reform? Ten Years of Transition, World Bank Annual Conference on Development Economics. Keynote Address. Washington, D.C., April 28-30, 1999.

(http://www.worldbank.org/research/abcde/pdfs/stiglitz.pd
f)

Secondary Material

- Abel, Istvan and Bonin, John P.: Financial Sector Reform in the Economies in Transition: On the Way to Privatizing Commercial Banks. In John P. Bonin and Istvan P. Szekely: *The Development and Reform of Financial Systems in Central and Eastern Europe*. England: Edward Elgar Publishing Limited, 1994.
- Abel, Istvan and Szekely, Istvan: Market Structures and Competition in the Hungarian Banking System. In John P. Bonin and Istvan P. Szekely: *The Development and Reform of Financial Systems in Central and Eastern Europe*. England: Edward Elgar Publishing Limited, 1994.
- Aghion, Philippe, Bolton, Patrick and Fries, Steven: Optimal design of bank bailouts: the case of transition economics. EBRD Working Paper 32, September 1998.
- Anderson, Ronald W. and Kegels, Chantal: *Transition Banking, Financial Development of Central and Eastern Europe*. United States: Oxford University Press Inc., 1998.
- Backe, Peter: Discussion on Eva Varhegyi's, The 'Second' Reform of the Hungarian Banking System. In Bonin & Szekely, *The Development and Reform of Financial Systems in Central and Eastern Europe*. England: Edward Elgar Publishing Limited, 1994.
- Balcerowicz, Leszek: *Socialism Capitalism Transformation*. Budapest: Central European Press, 1995.
- Begg, David and Portes, Richard: Enterprise debt and economic transformation: financial restructuring in Central and Eastern Europe. In Mayer & Vives: *Capital markets and financial institutions*. Cambridge: Cambridge University Press, 1992.
- Berglof, Erik and Roland, Gerard: Bank Restructuring and Soft Budget Constraints in Financial Transition. London: Centre for Economic Policy Research. Discussion Paper No. 1250 (November 1995).

■ Bonin, John P. and Szekely, Istvan P.: *The Development and Reform of Financial Systems in Central and Eastern Europe.* England: Edward Elgar Publishing Limited, 1994.

■ Boot, W.A. Arnoud and van Wijnbergen, Sweder: Financial Sector Design, regulation and Deposit Insurance in Eastern Europe. In Rostowski, Jacek: *Banking Reform in Central and Eastern Europe and the Former Soviet Union.* Budapest: Central European University Press, 1995.

■ Brada, Joseph: Privatization Is Transition - Or Is It? *Journal of Economic Perspectives* - Volume 10, Number 2 - Spring 1996.

■ Buiter, Willem H., Lago, Ricardo and Rey, Helen: Financing transition: investing in enterprises during macroeconomic transition. EBRD Working Paper No. 35, December 1998.

■ Corbett, Jenny and Mayer, Colin: Financial Reform in Eastern Europe: Progress with the Wrong Model. *Oxford Review of Economic Policy*, Vol. 7, No. 4, ~1991.

■ de Juan, Aristobulo: "False Friends" in Banking Reform. In Steven Fries: Building sound banking in transition economies. EBRD Working Paper No. 17, 1996.

■ Dittus, Peter (1994): Bank reform and behavior in Central Europe. *Journal of Comparative economics* 19.

■ *The Economist*, 29 July 2000.

■ European Bank for Reconstruction and Development: *Transition report update. United Kingdom*: EBRD Publications, April 1999.

■ European Bank for Reconstruction and Development: *Transition report 1998—Financial sector in transition.* United Kingdom: EBRD Publications, 1998.

■ European Bank for Reconstruction and Development: *Transition report 1997—Enterprise performance and growth.* United Kingdom: EBRD Publications, 1997.

■ European Bank for Reconstruction and Development: *Transition report 1995—Investment and enterprise development.* United Kingdom: EBRD Publications, 1995.

■ Enoch, Charles, Garcia, Gillian and Sundararajan, V.: Recapitalizing Banks with Public Funds: Selected Issues. IMF Working Paper WP/99/139, 1999.

- Erdely, Gabor: Development of Hungarian Banking: Outlook and Actions to Establish a Reliable System. In Steven Fries: Building sound banking in transition economies. EBRD Working Paper No. 17, 1996.
- Estrin, Saul: Economic transition and privatization: The issues. In Saul Estrin (Ed.): Privatization in Central an Eastern Europe. London, Longman. 1994.
- *George* magazine, Volume V Number 7, August 2000.
- Gray, Cheryl W. and Holle, Arnold: Bank-led restructuring in Poland (II): bankruptcy and it alternatives. *Economics of Transition*, Volume 5 (2), 1996.
- Gray, Cheryl W. and Holle, Arnold: Bank-led restructuring in Poland: the conciliation process in action. *Economics of Transition*, Volume 4 (2), 1996.
- Hexter, David: Transformation of Banking. In Steven Fries: Building sound banking in transition economies. EBRD Working Paper No. 17, 1996.
- Krugman, Paul and Obstfelt, Maurice: *International Economics Theory and Policy.* Reading, Massachusetts: Addison-Wesley, 1997.
- Lago, Ricardo: Macroeconomic Stabilization, Systemic Transformation and Bank Solvency. In Steven Fries: Building sound banking in transition economies. EBRD Working Paper No. 17, 1996.
- Lavigne, Marie: *The Economics of Transition—From Socialist Economy to Market Economy.* London: Macmillan Press Ltd., 1999.
- Mizsei, Kalman: Lessons from Bad Loan Management in the East Central European Economic Transition for the Second Wave of Reform Countries. In Jacek Rostowski: *Banking Reform in Central and Eastern Europe and the Former Soviet Union.* Budapest: Central European University Press, 1995.
- Murrell, Peter: How Far Has the Transition Progressed? *Journal of Economic Perspectives* - Volume 10, Number 2 - Spring 1996.
- Quinn, Brian: Banking Supervision in the Transition Economy. In Steven Fries: Building sound banking in transition economies. EBRD Working Paper No. 17, April 1996.

■ Rosati, Dariusz K.: The Polish Experience. In Steven Fries: Transition: private sector development and the role of financial institutions. EBRD Working Paper No.13, July 1994.

■ Rostowski, Jacek: *Banking Reform in Central and Eastern Europe and the Former Soviet Union.* Budapest: Central European University Press, 1995.

■ Stark, David and Bruszt, Laszlo: *Post Socialist Pathways—Transforming Politics and Property in East Central Europe.* United Kingdom: Cambridge University Press, 1998.

■ Stern, Nicholas: Introduction. In Steven Fries: Transition: private sector development and the role of financial institutions. EBRD Working Paper No.13, July 1994.

■ Stiglitz, Joseph: *Whither Socialism?* Cambridge, Massachusetts: MIT Press, 1994, p.208.

■ Varhegyi, Eva: The 'Second' Reform of the Hungarian Banking System. In Bonin & Szekely, *The Development and Reform of Financial Systems in Central and Eastern Europe.* England: Edward Elgar Publishing Limited, 1994.

■ World Bank: *World Development Report 1996—From Plan to Market.* New York: Oxford University Press. 1996.

James C. Mitchell, Jr.

About the Author:

James Mitchell was the Managing Director of International Sales and Marketing for CSX Corporation. In addition to his responsibilities at the corporate headquarters, Mr. Mitchell managed the company's offices in Europe and Latin America. He has two master's degrees from the London School of Economics and Northwestern University and a bachelor's degree from John Carroll University. Mr. Mitchell is a member of the Global Economy Network and the European Institute in London. Originally from Detroit, Michigan, he and his family currently live in Jacksonville, Florida.